HUMPTY DUMPTY'S FAVOURITE NURSERY RHYMES

Humpty Dumpty's Favourite Nursery Rhymes

Dawn and Peter Cope

TREASURE PRESS

Acknowledgements

We would like to acknowledge the following publishers who have granted us permission to use their copyright material in this book:

A & C Black for permission to reproduce the work of Charles Folkard and Dorothy Wheeler.

The Medici Society for permission to reproduce work by Margaret Tarrant.

The Oxford University Press for permission to reproduce work by Lilian Govey and Millicent Sowerby.

E T W Dennis for permission to reproduce the illustration by Anne Anderson.

J Salmon for permission to reproduce work by Flora White from their book **Favourite Nursery Rhymes.**

To Frederick Warne for permission to reproduce work by Randolph Caldecott.

To Valentines of Dundee and their archive holders, St Andrew's University, for permission to reproduce work by J Carleton-Smyth.

Every effort has been made to contact the true copyright holders of work reproduced in this book, and in case of error or omission the copyright holder is requested to contact Webb & Bower Limited.

First published in Great Britain in 1981 by Webb & Bower (Publishers) Ltd

Designed by Cope and Davies Ltd

This edition published in 1983 by Treasure Press 59 Grosvenor Street London W1

© 1981 Webb & Bower (Publishers) Ltd

ISBN 0 907812 51 1

Printed in Hong Kong

Contents

Introduction 6
Humpty Dumpty 9
Tom, Tom, the Piper's Son 10
Three Blind Mice 11
Ding Dong Bell 12
There Was a Little Man 13
I had a Little Sister 14
Old Mother Twitchet 15
Cock-a-Doodle-Doo 16
Little Tommy Tucker 17
Mary, Mary, Quite Contrary 18
Pat-a-Cake 19
A Frog He would A-wooing Go 20
To Market, To Market 23
Roses are Red 24
Little Boy Blue 25
Where are You Going to, My Pretty Maid? 26
Little Bo-Peep 28
I Love Little Pussy 29
Sing a Song of Sixpence 30
Old King Cole 31
There was an Old Woman who Lived in a Shoe 32
I Had a Little Nut Tree 33
Ride a Cock Horse 34
Goosey, Goosey Gander 35
Little Jack Horner 36
The Queen of Hearts 37
Handy Spandy, Jack-a-Dandy 38
Three Wise Men of Gotham 39
Pussy Cat, Pussy Cat 40
Curly Locks, Curly Locks 41
Hey Diddle Diddle 42
Jack Sprat 43
See-saw, Margery Daw 44
Ring-a-ring o' Roses 45
Simple Simon 46
Jack and Jill 47
If I had a Donkey 48
What are Little Boys Made of? 49
Oranges and Lemons 50
Baa, Baa, Black Sheep 51
Old Mother Hubbard 52
Blow, Wind, Blow 54
There was an Old Woman Tossed up in a Basket 55
The North Wind doth Blow 56
Tom, He was a Piper's Son 57
This is the House that Jack Built 58
Little Miss Muffett 61
I Saw Three Ships 62
Girls and Boys Come Out to Play 63
List of Illustrators 64

Introduction

When picture postcard publishers started to think seriously about themes to capture a child's imagination, it is no surprise that they should have chosen the nursery rhyme—the traditional language of childhood. They could be sure adults would buy them to send to their nieces and nephews or grandchildren, remembering the same rhymes they enjoyed during their own childhood. Of course children would want them too, for sending messages to their friends.

Ever since nursery rhymes have been printed it has been quite customary to illustrate them. Until the middle of the nineteenth century they were illustrated with simple wood or steel engravings, but the introduction of colour printing on a commercial scale gave illustrators scope and freedom to develop more varied styles and techniques of illustration.

Pictures are, after all, of paramount importance in books for the very young, as Iona and Peter Opie observe in *The Oxford Dictionary of Nursery Rhymes*:

"When reading to our children we have repeatedly found that a rhyme in a nursery rhyme book is uninteresting to a child unless it is accompanied by an illustration. The child looks at the sea of print and says 'Nothing on that page', meaning that there are no pictures on that page, and he turns over until he comes to a picture . . .".

Original and worthy themes for children's projects are always emerging, but none has eclipsed the traditional nursery rhyme for popularity, the theme which has been implanted in the minds of us all at an early and impressionable age.

Like fairy tales, nursery rhymes have been passed down by word of mouth through generations, their origins stretching back to mediaeval times—which is why we find today many variants of the same rhyme. Often the cards chosen for this book will show rhymes worded differently from the versions we use now.

Although books of infant rhymes had been published during the eighteenth and nineteenth centuries, the first comprehensive collection of nursery rhymes was *The Nursery Rhymes of England* by James Halliwell in 1842, followed by his *Popular Rhymes and Nursery Tales* in 1849.

By the 1870s and 80s, so great was the demand for books of nursery rhymes that many of the famous Victorian children's artists, including Kate Greenaway and Randolph Caldicott had illustrated them.

By the end of the century the popularity of nursery rhymes was such that they were printed on to all types of nursery items imaginable, including paper ephemera, greetings cards, building bricks, china, fabrics and furnishings.

The year 1900 brought with it the relaxing of postal regulations and the dawn of mass travel. These factors helped to create the craze for picture postcards. People were sending and collecting cards on all kinds of subjects—animal and flower studies, stage celebrities, heraldry, disasters, novelties with glitter and beauties with large pearly teeth.

Children were, of course, well catered for. Publishers brought out all the favourite children's themes: games and pastimes, scenes from fairyland, fairy tales and many more.

The first year that nursery rhymes were published on postcards was

A typical set of postcards with envelope.

1903 advertisement for postcards including nursery rhymes, see pages 19 and 47.

probably 1902, and during that year nearly all the prominent publishers of illustrated cards produced a series of their own. It is remarkable that all this should occur only sixty years after Halliwell with his first anthology had popularized nursery rhymes in print. Nursery rhyme postcards contain a fascinating variety of illustration styles. The early designs by Victorian artists were beautifully printed in up to sixteen separate colours. Every aspect of the production demonstrates the highest standards of craftsmanship, from the artist through to the printer. 'I Love Little Pussy' by Helen Jackson (*c.* 1905) on page 29 of this book is a fine example. Likewise, in 1903 a set of six rhymes by Jessie M. King (1875–1949), a renowned artist of the Glasgow School of Art, was issued, the only series of postcards she ever illustrated. Unmistakably Art Nouveau, the designs were uniquely produced on 'watered silk' paper—see 'The Queen of Hearts' on page 37.

Linda Edgerton (*b.* 1890) whose stylized work appears on pages 14, 15 23 and 58, was the most prolific illustrator of nursery rhymes on postcards. Between 1914 and 1920 she illustrated at least twelve different series of six cards. She illustrated several series of fairy tales as well, which are featured in the companion volume to this book.

Introduction

The Oxford University Press was a prominent publisher of books for the very young around the 1920s, and brought out over seventy sets of children's postcards under the series title *Postcards for the Little Ones*, highlighting all the popular children's themes. They commissioned successful children's illustrators of the day like Millicent Sowerby (1878–1967), Lilian Govey (1886–1974) and Susan Beatrice Pearse (1878–1980), who was the creator of the popular *Ameliaranne* series of books. Their illustrations, so evocative of the 'twenties and 'thirties, were characterized by the unchanging basics of children's fashions at the time—smocked dresses, bar shoes and little boys in shorts.

Sometimes publishers reproduced book illustrations as postcards, not only for greater revenue but also to help promote the book.

Many fine book illustrations were issued as postcards by A & C Black, such as, 'Three Blind Mice' from *Mother Goose Nursery Rhymes* (1919) by

Charles Folkard on page 11 and 'A Frog He would A-wooing Go', one of thirty from *English Nursery Rhymes* (1915) by Dorothy Wheeler, page 20.

Illustrations which were published in books before the dawn of postcards were sometimes issued again much later by postcard publishers, such as illustrations from *Mother Goose* by Kate Greenaway (1881) and *Randolph Caldecott's Picture Books* (1878–1886) (see examples on pages 26 and 27).

Postcards were the best way of conveying a quick message before the advent of the telephone. Generally they cost one old penny when new and could be mailed for a halfpenny (rising to one penny after 1918, unless the message was compressed into five words or less). Frequently they would have been sent to the younger members of the family by the older members. What better than to buy a packet of six nursery rhyme postcards to send at regular intervals? They knew that a nursery picture with a little message would be sure to delight.

Christmas postcard by Agnes Richardson (c. 1920)

There are often touching messages on the backs of old postcards, like this:

"This little boy is fishing in a pail, but I don't think he is going to catch his lunch. His name is Simple Simon. Fondest love Grandma."

Or this:

"Please thank Mummie for her postcard and ask her to take you and Angela to have a nice ice & some cakes from Auntie Doll. Lots of love."

Or simply:

"Love and kisses from Daddy."

The rhymes most favoured by publishers and artists of postcards were the ever-popular 'Little Miss Muffett', 'Little Bo-peep', 'Little Boy Blue', 'Tom, Tom, the Piper's Son', 'Mary, Mary, Quite Contrary' and 'Jack and Jill'—rhymes which would be sure to appeal, as they have always been amongst the best in the nursery.

What pleasure picture postcards must have given, and it is sad that increasing postal charges and telephone ownership during the 'thirties diminished their popularity.

A selection of children's books with postcards reproduced from them.

*H*umpty Dumpty sat on a wall,
  Humpty Dumpty had a great fall.
All the King's horses and all the King's men,
Couldn't put Humpty together again.

Best Wishes for Christmas

*T*om, Tom, the piper's son,
Stole a pig and away he run.
The pig was eat
And Tom was beat,
And Tom went roaring down the street.

Three Blind Mice

*T*hree blind mice, three blind mice,
See how they run, see how they run!
They all ran after the farmer's wife,
Who cut off their tails with a carving knife,
Did ever you see such a thing in your life,
As three blind mice?

DING, DONG, BELL!

Ding, dong, bell! Pussy's in the well!
Who put her in? Little Johnny Green.

Who pull'd her out?
Big Tommy Stout.

Ding dong bell,
Pussy's in the well.
Who put her in?
Little Johnny Green.
Who pulled her out?
Little Tommy Stout.
What a naughty boy was that
To try to drown poor pussy cat,
Who never did him any harm,
But killed the mice in his father's barn.

There was a Little Man

Nursery Rhymes Illustrated.

THERE WAS A LITTLE MAN & HE HAD A LITTLE GUN.

There was a little man and he had a little gun,
*   And his bullets were made of lead, lead, lead.*
He went to the brook and he shot a little duck
*   Right through the middle of its head, head, head.*

He carried it home to his old wife Joan,
*   And bade her a fire for to make, make, make.*
To roast the little duck he had shot in the brook
*   And he'd go and fetch her the drake, drake, drake.*

I had a little sister her name was Pretty Peep,
She wades in the water deep deep deep,
She climbs up the mountains high high high,
My poor little sister has but one eye.

OLD MOTHER TWITCHET HAD BUT ONE EYE
AND A LONG TAIL WHICH SHE LET FLY
AND EVERY TIME SHE WENT OVER A GAP
SHE LEFT A BIT OF HER TAIL IN A TRAP

*O*ld Mother Twitchet had but one eye
And a long tail which she let fly,
And every time she went over a gap
She left a bit of her tail in a trap.

Cock-a-doodle-doo!
My dame has lost her shoe,
My master's lost his fiddling stick,
And doesn't know what to do.

Cock-a-doodle-doo!
What is my dame to do?
Till master finds his fiddling stick
She'll dance without her shoe.

Cock-a-doodle-doo!
My dame has lost her shoe,
And master's found his fiddling stick,
Sing doodle doodle doo.

Cock-a-doodle-doo!
My dame will dance with you,
While master finds his fiddling stick
For dame and doodle-doo!

Little Tommy Tucker
Sings for his supper.
What shall we give him?
Brown bread and butter.
How shall he cut it
Without e'er a knife?
How shall he marry
Without e'er a wife?

MISTRESS·MARY
MISTRESS·MARY,·QUITE·CONTRARY,
HOW·DOES·YOUR·GARDEN·GROW?

Mary, Mary, quite contrary,
How does your garden grow?
With silver bells and cockle shells,
And pretty maids all in a row.

"PAT A CAKE, PAT A CAKE, BAKERS MAN."

Pat-a-cake, pat-a-cake, baker's man,
Bake me a cake as fast as you can;
Pat it and prick it and mark it with T,
And put it in the oven for Tommy and me.

A Frog he would a-wooing go

A frog he would a-wooing go,
Heigh-ho, says Rowley.
Whether his mother would let him or no.
With a rowley, powley, gammon and spinach.
Heigh-ho, says Anthony Rowley.

A Frog He would A-wooing Go

So off he set with his opera hat,
  Heigh-ho, says Rowley.
And on the road he met with a rat.
  With a rowley, powley, gammon and spinach.
  Heigh-ho, says Anthony Rowley.

Pray Mr Rat, will you go with me?
  Heigh-ho, says Rowley.
Kind Mistress Mousey for to see?
  With a rowley, powley, gammon and spinach.
  Heigh-ho, says Anthony Rowley.

They came to the door of Mousey's hall.
  Heigh-ho, says Rowley.
They gave a loud knock and gave a loud call.
  With a rowley, powley, gammon and spinach.
  Heigh-ho, says Anthony Rowley.

Pray Mistress Mousey, are you within?
  Heigh-ho, says Rowley.
Oh yes, kind sirs, I'm sitting to spin.
  With a rowley, powley, gammon and spinach.
  Heigh-ho, says Anthony Rowley.

Pray Mistress Mousey, will you give us some beer?
  Heigh-ho, says Rowley.
For Froggy and I are fond of good cheer.
  With a rowley, powley, gammon and spinach.
  Heigh-ho, says Anthony Rowley.

Pray Mr Frog, will you give us a song?
  Heigh-ho, says Rowley.
Let it be something that's not very long.
  With a rowley, powley, gammon and spinach.
  Heigh-ho, says Anthony Rowley.

A Frog He would A-wooing Go

But while they were all a-merry-making,
   Heigh-ho, says Rowley.
A cat and her kittens came tumbling in.
   With a rowley, powley, gammon and spinach.
   Heigh-ho, says Anthony Rowley.

The cat she seized the rat by the crown.
   Heigh-ho, says Rowley.
The kittens they pulled the little mouse down.
   With a rowley, powley, gammon and spinach.
   Heigh-ho, says Anthony Rowley.

This put Mr Frog in a terrible fright.
   Heigh-ho, says Rowley.
He took up his hat and wished them goodnight.
   With a rowley, powley, gammon and spinach.
   Heigh-ho, says Anthony Rowley.

But as Froggy was crossing over a brook,
   Heigh-ho, says Rowley.
A lily-white duck came and gobbled him up.
   With a rowley, powley, gammon and spinach.
   Heigh-ho, says Anthony Rowley.

So there was the end of one, two, three.
   Heigh-ho, says Rowley.
The rat, the mouse and the little frog-ee.
   With a rowley, powley, gammon and spinach.
   Heigh-ho, says Anthony Rowley.

To Market, To Market

To market, to market,
To buy a plum bun.
Home again, home again,
Market is done.

To market, to market,
To buy a fat pig.
Home again, home again,
Jiggety jig.

To market, to market,
To buy a fat hog.
Home again, home again,
Joggety jog.

THE·ROSE·IS·RED·
THE·VIOLET'S·BLUE·
THE·CARNATION'S·SWEET
AND·SO·ARE·YOU;·

*L*ilies are white,
Rosemary's green,
When I am king,
   You shall be queen.

Roses are red,
   Violets are blue,
Sugar is sweet
   And so are you.

LITTLE BOY BLUE

Little Boy Blue, come blow on your horn
The sheep's in the meadow, the cow's in the corn ;
But where is the boy that looks after the sheep ;
Under a haystack fast asleep.

*L*ittle Boy Blue,
  Come blow up your horn,
The sheep's in the meadow,
  The cow's in the corn.
Where is the boy
  Who looks after the sheep?
He's under the haycock fast asleep.
  Will you wake him? No, not I,
For if I do he's sure to cry.

W*here are you going to, my pretty maid?*
I'm going a-milking, sir, she said,
Sir, she said, sir, she said,
I'm going a-milking, sir, she said.

May I go with you, my pretty maid?
You're kindly welcome, sir, she said,
Sir, she said, sir, she said,
You're kindly welcome, sir, she said.

What is your father, my pretty maid?
My father's a farmer, sir, she said,
Sir, she said, sir, she said,
My father's a farmer, sir, she said.

"Then I can't marry you, my pretty Maid!"

—The Milkmaid—

From the Original Drawing by RANDOLPH CALDECOTT

PUBLISHED BY F. WARNE & Cº

Say, will you marry me, my pretty maid?
Yes, if you please, kind sir, she said,
Sir, she said, sir, she said,
Yes, if you please, kind sir, she said.

What is your fortune, my pretty maid?
My face is my fortune, sir, she said,
Sir, she said, sir, she said,
My face is my fortune, sir, she said.

Then I can't marry you, my pretty maid.
Nobody asked you, sir, she said,
Sir, she said, sir, she said,
Nobody asked you, sir, she said.

Little Bo-Peep who lost her sheep
And could'nt tell where to find them.
Left them alone and they came home,
But they'd left their tails behind 'em.

*L*ittle Bo-peep has lost her sheep,
 And doesn't know where to find them.
Leave them alone, and they'll come home,
 Bringing their tails behind them.

Little Bo-peep fell fast asleep,
 And dreamt she heard them bleating,
But when she awoke, she found it a joke,
 For still they were a-fleeting.

I love little pussy,
Her coat is so warm,
And if I don't hurt her
She'll do me no harm.

So I won't pull her tail,
Nor drive her away,
And pussy and I
Very gently will play.

She shall sit by my side,
And I'll give her some food,
And pussy will love me
Because I am good.

Sing a song of sixpence,
   A pocket full of rye;
Four and twenty blackbirds,
   Baked in a pie.

When the pie was opened,
   The birds began to sing;
Wasn't that a dainty dish,
   To set before the king?

The king was in his counting-house,
   Counting out his money;
The queen was in the parlour,
   Eating bread and honey.

The maid was in the garden,
   Hanging out the clothes,
When down came a blackbird
   And pecked off her nose.

Old King Cole was a merry old soul,
And a merry old soul was he.
He called for his pipe
And he called for his bowl,
And he called for his fiddlers three.

Every fiddler had a very fine fiddle
And a very fine fiddle had he;
Oh, there's none so rare
As can compare
With King Cole and his fiddlers three.

There was an old woman
Who lived in a shoe.
She had so many children,
She didn't know what to do.
So she gave them some broth
Without any bread,
Then whipped them all soundly
And sent them to bed.

I had a little nut tree,
  Nothing would it bear
But a silver nutmeg
  And a golden pear.

The King of Spain's daughter
  Came to visit me,
And all for the sake
  Of my little nut tree.

I skipped over water,
  I danced over sea,
And all the birds in the air
  Couldn't catch me.

RIDE A COCK-HORSE.
Ride a cock horse to Banbury Cross,
See a fine lady get on a white horse
Rings on her fingers and Bells on her toes
She shall have music wherever she goes.

Ride a cock horse
To Banbury Cross,
To see a fine lady
Upon a white horse.
Rings on her fingers
And bells on her toes,
And she shall have music
Wherever she goes.

Goosey, goosey gander,
Whither shall I wander?
Upstairs and downstairs
   And in my lady's chamber.
There I met an old man
   Who wouldn't say his prayers,
So I took him by the left leg
   And threw him down the stairs.

LITTLE · JACK · HORNER ·
LITTLE · JACK HORNER · SAT · IN · A · CORNER.
EATING · HIS · CHRISTMAS · PIE.

Little Jack Horner
Sat in the corner,
Eating a Christmas pie.
He put in his thumb,
And pulled out a plum,
And said, What a good boy am I!

THE·QUEEN·OF·HEARTS·SHE·BAKED·SOME·TARTS·ALL·ON·A·SUMMER·DAY·

The Queen of Hearts
She made some tarts,
All on a summer's day.
The Knave of Hearts
He stole those tarts,
And took them clean away.

The King of Hearts
Called for the tarts,
And beat the knave full sore.
The Knave of Hearts
Brought back the tarts,
And vowed he'd steal no more.

HANDY
SPANDY
JACK-
A-DANDY

FOR INSTRUCTIONS
SEE OTHER SIDE

*H*andy Spandy, Jack-a-Dandy,
  Loved plum cake and sugar candy.
He bought some at a grocer's shop,
And out he came, hop, hop, hop, hop.

T hree wise men of Gotham
  Went to sea in a bowl.
If the bowl had been stronger,
My song would have been longer.

*P*ussy cat, pussy cat,
   Where have you been?
I've been to London
   To look at the Queen.
Pussy cat, pussy cat
   What did you there?
I frightened a little mouse
   Under the chair.

Curly Locks

Curly Locks Curly Locks, wilt thou be mine?
Thou shalt not wash dishes nor yet feed the swine
But sit on a cushion and sew a fine seam,
And live upon strawberries, sugar and cream!

*C*urly locks, curly locks,
Wilt thou be mine?
Thou shalt not wash the dishes
Nor yet feed the swine.
But sit on a cushion
And sew a fine seam,
And feed upon strawberries,
Sugar and cream.

*H*ey diddle diddle,
  The cat and the fiddle,
The cow jumped over the moon.
The little dog laughed
To see such sport,
And the dish ran away with the spoon.

Jack Sprat

Jack Spratt could eat no *Fat*
His *Wife* could eat no *Lean*
And so betwixt them both you see
They licked the *Platter* clean

*J*ack Sprat could eat no fat,
  His wife could eat no lean,
And so betwixt them both, you see,
  They licked the platter clean.

See saw Marjory Daw
Johnny shall have a
new Master

*S*ee-saw, Margery Daw,
 Johnny shall have a new master.
He shall have but a penny a day,
Because he can't work any faster.

*R*ing-a-ring o' roses,
A pocket full of posies,
A-tishoo! A-tishoo!
We all fall down.

Simple Simon met a pieman,
  Going to the fair.
Says Simple Simon to the pieman,
  Let me taste your ware.

Says the pieman to Simple Simon,
  Show me first your penny.
Says Simple Simon to the pieman,
  Indeed I have not any.

Simple Simon went a-fishing
  For to catch a whale.
But all the water he had got
  Was in his mother's pail.

Simple Simon went to look
  If plums grew on a thistle.
He pricked his finger very much,
  Which made poor Simon whistle.

"JACK AND JILL,
WENT UP A HILL."

Jack and Jill went up the hill
 To fetch a pail of water.
Jack fell down and broke his crown,
 And Jill came tumbling after.

Up Jack got, and home did trot,
 As fast as he could caper,
To old Dame Dob, who patched his nob
 With vinegar and brown paper.

IF I HAD A DONKEY

If I had a Donkey, and he wouldn't go,
Do you think I'd beat him? Oh, no, no!

I'd put him in a stable and give him some corn:
The best little Donkey that ever was born.

If I had a donkey
That wouldn't go,
Would I beat him?
Oh no, no.
I'd put him in the barn
And give him some corn,
The best little donkey
That ever was born.

WHAT ARE LITTLE BOYS MADE OF?

WHAT ARE LITTLE BOYS MADE OF?   SLUGS AND SNAILS AND PUPPY-DOGS' TAILS;
WHAT ARE LITTLE BOYS MADE OF?   THAT'S WHAT LITTLE BOYS ARE MADE OF.

What are little boys made of?
What are little boys made of?
  Slugs and snails
   And puppy-dogs' tails,
That's what little boys are made of.

What are little girls made of?
What are little girls made of?
  Sugar and spice
   And all that's nice,
That's what little girls are made of.

Oranges and lemons,
Say the bells of St Clement's.
You owe me five farthings,
Say the bells of St Martin's.
When will you pay me?
Say the bells at Old Bailey.

When I grow rich,
Say the bells at Shoreditch.
When will that be?
Say the bells at Stepney.
I'm sure I don't know,
Says the great bell at Bow.

Here comes a candle to light you to bed,
Here comes a chopper to chop off your head.
Chip, chop, chip, chop. The last man's dead.

Baa, Baa, Black Sheep

Baa, baa, black sheep,
Have you any wool?
Yes sir, yes sir,
    Three bags full.
One for the master
    And one for the dame,
And one for the little boy
    Who lives down the lane.

Old Mother Hubbard

Old Mother Hubbard

O ld Mother Hubbard
Went to the cupboard,
To fetch her poor dog a bone,
But when she got there
The cupboard was bare
And so the poor dog had none.

Old Mother Hubbard

She went to the baker's
　To buy him some bread,
But when she came back
　The poor dog was dead.

She went to the joiner's
　To buy him a coffin,
But when she came back
　The poor dog was laughing.

She took a clean dish
　To get him some tripe,
But when she came back
　He was smoking a pipe.

She went to the seamstress
　To buy him some linen,
But when she came back
　The dog was a-spinning.

She went to the fruiterer's
　To buy him some fruit,
But when she came back
　He was playing the flute.

She went to the hatter's
　To buy him a hat,
But when she came back
　He was feeding the cat.

She went to the tailor's
　To buy him a coat,
But when she came back
　He was riding a goat.

She went to the barber's
　To buy him a wig
But when she came back
　He was dancing a jig.

She went to the cobbler's
　To buy him some shoes,
But when she came back
　He was reading the news.

She went to the fish shop
　To buy him some fish,
But when she came back
　He was washing the dish.

She went to the tavern
　For white wine and red,
But when she came back
　He stood on his head.

She went to the hosier's
　To buy him some hose,
But when she came back
　He was dressed up in clothes.

The dame made a curtsey,
The dog made a bow,
The dame said, Your servant
The dog said, Bow-wow.

Blow, wind, blow, and go, mill, go,
That the miller may grind his corn :
That the baker may take it,
And into bread bake it,
And bring us a loaf in the morn.

*Blow, wind, blow!
And go mill, go!
That the miller may grind his corn.
That the baker may take it,
And into bread make it,
And bring us a loaf in the morn.*

*T*here was an old woman tossed up in a blanket
Seventeen times as high as the moon.
And where she was going I couldn't but ask it,
    For in her hand she carried a broom.
Old woman, old woman, old woman, quoth I,
    O whither, O whither, O whither so high?
To sweep the cobwebs off the sky!
    Shall I go with you? Aye, by-and-by.

THE NORTH WIND DOTH BLOW.

The north wind doth blow.
And we shall have snow,

And what will poor Robin
do then, poor thing?

The north wind doth blow,
And we shall have snow,
And what will poor Robin do then?
Poor thing.
He'll sit in a barn,
And keep himself warm,
And hide his head under his wing,
Poor thing.

Tom, He was a Piper's Son

TOM WAS A PIPER'S SON.

Tom he was a piper's son,
He learned to play when he was young,

But all the tunes that he could play
Was " Over the hills and far away."

*T*om, he was a piper's son,
He learnt to play when he was young,
But all the tunes that he could play
Was, Over the hills and far away,
Over the hills and a great way off,
The wind shall blow my top-knot off.

Now Tom with his pipe made such a noise,
That he pleased both the girls and boys,
And they all stopped to hear him play,
Over the hills and far away.

THIS·IS·THE
HOUSE·THAT
JACK·BUILT·

This is the house that Jack built.

This is the malt
That lay in the house that Jack built.

This is the rat,
That ate the malt
That lay in the house that Jack built.

This is the House that Jack Built

This is the cat,
That killed the rat,
That ate the malt
That lay in the house that Jack built.

This is the dog,
That worried the cat,
That killed the rat,
That ate the malt
That lay in the house that Jack built.

This is the cow with the crumpled horn,
That tossed the dog,
That worried the cat,
That killed the rat,
That ate the malt
That lay in the house that Jack built.

This is the maiden all forlorn,
That milked the cow with crumpled horn,
That tossed the dog,
That worried the cat,
That killed the rat,
That ate the malt
That lay in the house that Jack built.

This is the man all tattered and torn,
That kissed the maiden all forlorn,
That milked the cow with the crumpled horn,
That tossed the dog,
That worried the cat,
That killed the rat,
That ate the malt
That lay in the house that Jack built.

This is the priest all shaven and shorn,
That married the man all tattered and torn,
That kissed the maiden all forlorn,
That milked the cow with the crumpled horn,
That tossed the dog,
That worried the cat,
That killed the rat,
That ate the malt
That lay in the house that Jack built.

This is the cock that crowed in the morn,
That waked the priest all shaven and shorn,
That married the man all tattered and torn,
That kissed the maiden all forlorn,
That milked the cow with the crumpled horn,
That tossed the dog,
That worried the cat,
That killed the rat,
That ate the malt
That lay in the house that Jack built.

This is the farmer sowing his corn,
That kept the cock that crowed in the morn,
That waked the priest all shaven and shorn,
That married the man all tattered and torn,
That kissed the maiden all forlorn,
That milked the cow with the crumpled horn,
That tossed the dog,
That worried the cat,
That killed the rat,
That ate the malt
That lay in the house that Jack built.

Little Miss Muffett
Sat on a tuffet,
Eating her curds and whey.
There came a big spider,
Who sat down beside her
And frightened Miss Muffett away.

I Saw Three Ships

I saw Three Ships
come sailing in
On Christmas Day,
on Christmas Day,
I saw Three Ships
come sailing in
On Christmas Day
in the Morning.
OLD CAROL

I saw three ships come sailing by,
Come sailing by, come sailing by,
I saw three ships come sailing by,
On Christmas Day in the morning.

What do you think was in them then,
Was in them then, was in them then?
What do you think was in them then,
On Christmas Day in the morning?

Three pretty girls were in them then,
Were in them then, were in them then,
Three pretty girls were in them then,
On Christmas Day in the morning.

One could whistle, and one could sing,
And one could play the violin.
Such joy there was at my wedding,
On Christmas Day in the morning.

GIRLS AND BOYS, COME OUT TO PLAY

1. { Girls and boys, come out to play, The moon doth shine as bright as day; }
   { Leave your supper and lose your sleep, And come with your playfellows into the street }

CHORUS

Come with a whoop, come with a call, ... Come with a good-will, or not at all

*G*irls and boys come out to play,
The moon doth shine as bright as day.
Leave your supper and leave your sleep,
And join your playfellows in the street.
Come with a whoop and come with a call,
Come with a good will or not at all.
Up the ladder and down the wall,
A half-penny loaf will serve us all.
You find milk and I'll find flour
And we'll have a pudding in half an hour.

List of Illustrators

9 *Dorothy Wheeler (1915)*
10 *Cecil Aldin (1898)*
11 *Charles Folkard (1911)*
12 *A E Kennedy (1918)*
13 *John Hassall (1904)*
14 *Linda Edgerton (1919)*
15 *Linda Edgerton (1919)*
16 *Joyce Mercer (1925)*
17 *Flora White (1915)*
18 *Millicent Sowerby (1919)*
19 *Anon (1903)*
20 *Dorothy Wheeler (1915)*
23 *Linda Edgerton (1918)*
24 *Anne Anderson (1917)*
25 *Margaret Tarrant (1925)*
26 *Randolph Caldecott (1881)*
27 *Randolph Caldecott (1881)*
28 *Ethel Parkinson (1911)*
29 *Helen Jackson (c1904)*
30 *D Carleton-Smyth (c1903)*
31 *Anon (1903)*
32 *Lilian Govey (c1922)*
33 *Sybil Barham (1921)*
34 *Agnes Richardson (c1924)*
35 *Anon (1903)*
36 *Millicent Sowerby (1919)*
37 *Jessie M King (1903)*
38 *Anon (1922)*
39 *Joyce Mercer (1925)*
40 *Anon (c1908)*
41 *Helen Marsh Lambert (1912)*
42 *Anon (1904)*
43 *Stanley Rogers (c1913)*
44 *Will Kidd (c1910)*
45 *Alice Wanke (c1907)*
46 *Eugenie Richards (c1909)*
47 *Anon (1903)*
48 *A E Kennedy (1918)*
49 *Doris Bowden (1921)*
50 *Anne Anderson (c1912)*
51 *Dorothy Wheeler (1915)*
52 *Charles Folkard (1911)*
54 *Margaret Tarrant (1925)*
55 *Anon (1903)*
56 *Hilda Miller (1921)*
57 *Hilda Miller (1921)*
58 *Linda Edgerton (1918)*
61 *Anon (c1902)*
62 *Marion Miller (c1905)*
63 *Dorothy Wheeler (1915)*